BookRags Literature Study Guide

Bad Girls of the Bible
by Liz Curtis Higgs

Copyright Information

ISBN: 978-1-304-49082-7

Table of Contents

Plot Summary

In Bad Girls of the Bible: And What We Can Learn From Them, Liz Curtis Higgs examines the lives, situations, and personalities of ten Bad Girls from the Bible. She argues that many women may not connect as well with the Good Girls of the Bible, like Ruth, Mary, and Esther, because earthly women are sinful and mess up from time to time. The Bad Girls of the Bible give women who have their own pasts to deal with examples of what to do or not to do in their own lives. Higgs argues that while women can learn from the Good Girls, they can also learn from the Bad Girls of the Bible as well.

In this book, Higgs chooses ten Bad Girls to focus on. Some of these women play prominent roles in the Bible, while others are barely mentioned. Yet, Higgs argues that they each have something to teach the modern woman about what not to do, as well as how to live a better life in Christ. Higgs includes the following Bad Girls: Eve, Potiphar's wife, Lot's wife, the woman at the well, Delilah, Sapphira, Rahab, Jezebel, Michal, and the sinful woman. She identifies each of them as being bad to the bone, bad for a season, or bad for a moment.

In each chapter of the book, Higgs focuses on a different woman. She begins each chapter with a fictional account, set in modern times, that resembles the story from the Bible of the woman she's examining. Higgs weaves in the Biblical verses about the woman in question with theological commentary and her own thoughts on the situation and the woman herself. In doing so, she provides a greater context for the women, particularly for those that are not named in the Bible and only appear for a short time, such as Potiphar's wife, Lot's wife, and the sinful woman.

After her analysis of each Bad Girl, Higgs includes the lessons that modern women can take away from each Bad Girl. These lessons are designed to help today's women be better Christians, mothers, wives, and friends. Higgs talks about using these lessons to better follow Christ. She also includes a number of discussion questions for each Bad Girl, making the book a good choice for both individual and group reading. The questions are designed to get today's woman to consider how her life and actions are similar to the Bad Girls and how she she learn from their mistakes.

Introduction, Turn Signal Summary and Analysis

In Bad Girls of the Bible: And What We Can Learn From Them, Liz Curtis Higgs examines the lives, situations, and personalities of ten Bad Girls from the Bible. She argues that many women may not connect as well with the Good Girls of the Bible, like Ruth, Mary, and Esther, because earthly women are sinful and mess up from time to time. The Bad Girls of the Bible give women who have their own pasts to deal with examples of what to do or not to do in their own lives. Higgs argues that while women can learn from the Good Girls, they can also learn from the Bad Girls of the Bible as well.

Ruthie didn't see the fist coming toward her face until it was too late. She is nineteen and a good girl in her small town. She's never experienced something like this before. She'd met Hayden three weeks before and she'd brought him home with her that night.

Hayden tells Ruthie to get over in the car, her new car, so that he can drive. Ruthie slides across the seat, but puts a hand on the door handle. She shoves the door open and tumbles out. She hurries toward her apartment, hoping to lock herself inside, but Hayden manages to get part of his body in before she can lock the door. Hayden tells her that she is his, along with everything she owns.

Higgs writes that few women have the ambition to be a bad girl, but sometimes she stares back at us from the mirror. Badness can be dramatic, but it doesn't have to be. Sometimes it's just a small action or word, coming from a heart hardened against God.

Higgs has trouble learning from the women who get it right all the time, particularly since she falls short so often. So, she wants to look at the women of the Bible who got things wrong to see what they can teach the women of today. Her introduction to the Bad Girls began a number of years ago as she worked on messages for a national convention. When Higgs came across Jezebel, she found that she identified with aspects of the ultimate Bad Girl. Higgs understood her outbursts, need for control, and pushy personality. Throughout the Bible, she found other Bad Girls who helped teach her what not to do in her own life.

Higgs says that the good news is that God loves even the Bad Girls. He puts people in the path of the Bad Girl to lead her to God. That's what happened to Higgs herself long ago. Ruthie is Higgs' own story. Higgs was a Bad Girl who found her way.

Chapter 1, All About Evie Summary and Analysis

Evelyn has always loved her father's garden in Savannah. Her first memories are of being in the garden, and it is her father's pride and joy. Evelyn believes that her father created the garden to please her, even though he gets enjoyment from it too. Flowers and plants are all through the garden and a gazebo is at the center, although Evelyn has never actually seen the gazebo. Evelyn father had asked her to avoid the gazebo. Evelyn loves her father and it is easy to obey him on this. Her father had also told her fiancÃ© Adam to avoid the gazebo too.

Hours later, Evelyn is dressed in a beautiful gown. The party is small and exclusive and Adam Mann would be there. Both Adam and Evelyn love the outdoors and they often take strolls through the squares of Savannah. Adam is Evelyn's best friend and her future husband. As the party begins, Evelyn descends the steps to where Adam waits. Her father walks her down, and within a few minutes, Evelyn's introduction to society is complete. Evelyn and Adam dance along with the other couples.

Soon, Evelyn decides that she needs some air and she walks outside. She finds herself by a man in a black tuxedo. Evelyn finds the man attractive, although he looks nothing like Adam. The man's name is Devin and he asks if Evelyn is allowed to sit under all of the trees in the garden. She tells me that she is, but that her father has asked her to stay away from the gazebo.

Devin tells Evelyn that her father must know something that he doesn't want her to know. He guides her toward the gazebo without Evelyn even realizing it. Devin says that she'll discover something delicious in the gazebo. Evelyn sees the gazebo for the first time and thinks that it looks enchanting. She follows Devin inside, but it's different inside. Suddenly, the gazebo looks disappointing and the air seems warmer.

Devin kisses Evelyn and it tastes sweet to her. She's disobeyed her father but nothing bad has happened. She hears Adam's voice and calls out to him. When he comes to her, she kisses him as Devin had kissed her. She sees vulnerability in his eyes now and she begins to unbutton his shirt.

Suddenly, Evelyn's father appears. She feels panic and she sees her guilt mirrored in Adam's eyes. They realize that when Evelyn's father finds them that there will be hell to pay.

In the beginning, Adam and Eve were in the garden. God had carefully planned the garden and maintaining it was Adam's job. God told Adam not to eat from the tree of the knowledge of good and evil. Higgs says that while knowledge is good, an intimate knowledge of evil is not. God was trying to protect humans from evil.

Adam obeyed God, but he was lonely in the Garden all alone. Higgs argues that God created humans to be social, to connect with others. God first gave Adam pets, but these didn't work for Adam. So, God created woman from Adam's ribs. Higgs thinks that Eve must have been beautiful, as she would have had no scars, blemishes, or ugly inherited feet. Eve was also without sin and didn't have to worry about any real or perceived competition.

Then the serpent showed up. Different translations call him cunning, most clever, and sliest. The serpent approached Eve first and Higgs wonders why this is. The serpent waited until she was alone, and Eve didn't go get Adam because she knew that he'd talk her out of it. Satan twisted God's words and reeled Eve in. He steered the conversation away from God's word toward Eve's desires. He kept himself out of the conversation completely. Eve stopped looking toward God and goodness. The serpent just stepped back and left Eve to make the final decision herself.

Eve took her eyes off the good and put them on the forbidden. The fruit appealed to Eve, although it was probably not an actual apple. She wanted the shortcut to knowledge and wisdom. She could have even stopped with just touching the fruit, but she didn't. Many scholars have written about why Eve ate the fruit. She had the chance to remain innocent, but she chose to eat. The world changed forever when she did.

When Eve ate the fruit, there was no sudden drama or lightening bolts. She just ate. She had no one to blame but herself. At some point Adam showed up, although when in the process this happened isn't clear from the Bible. Higgs argues that we do know that he didn't protest Eve's suggestion that he eat as well. He became Eve's partner in sin, although Eve has the distinction of going first.

Higgs argues that if Adam had been offered the fruit instead of Eve that he would have taken it. Human nature is human nature and man is no less a sinner. So, Adam and Eve, partners in sin, now have to face God. They don't want to face God, just like humans today don't want to face God when they sin. Adam and Eve tried to deflect blame.

Higgs says that the lessons women can learn from Eve include not getting into a debate with Satan. Individuals should just get out of the situation. It's also important to know God's word so that one won't be fooled. Satan will try to hit women in their weaknesses so it's important to know what they are.

Higgs also says that women should avoid playing the blame game when they sin.

Chapter 2, Bored to Distraction Summary and Analysis

Mitzi leans toward her husband, trying to give him an eyeful of her cleavage. Her husband just continues to read the paper. Christopher didn't know how boring her days were, waiting for him to get home and notice her. Christopher mentions the new guy he's hired at the office. Joe is his name. Mitzi wonders if Christopher is really that blind that he didn't know she'd already noticed Joe.

Mitzi has heard the rumors that Joe is a do-gooder and religious. She just thinks that she needs a challenge in her life anyway. Christopher has left her alone too much and she thinks Joe will add a little pep to her life. Today, Christopher tells her that he'll be home late again.

After Christopher leaves, Mitzi makes a few calls, telling the gardener and housekeeper not to come. She calls her husband's company and asks for Joe. She tells him that she needs him to come get a file and cell phone that Christopher left behind. Joe tells her that he'll be right over.

Mitzi puts on perfume after she gets out of the tub. She also puts on a scarlet nightgown that leaves little to the imagination. When she hears his knock, she almost skips down the stairs. She tries to look innocent, although Joe still looks shocked when she opens the door. Mitzi pulls Joe into the house and offers him something to eat. He looks uncomfortable and she wonders if this will be harder than she thought. She finally asks if he knows why she invited him over and he says that he does now. However, Joe opens the door, saying that going to bed with her is a sin. He leaves.

13

Mitzi's mad and she feels foolish. She wonders if Joe will tell Christopher or one of the others at the office. Then she notices that Joe has left his jacket. She decides that she'll tell Christopher that Joe showed up and tried to force himself on her. Her husband will believe her over Joe. She calls Christopher's office, faking tears and fear.

The Old Testament also contains a story about a bored wife and a hired man. The wife doesn't even have a name; she's known only as Potiphar's wife. Her husband was the head of Pharaoh's security and was probably a big man. He was important and everyone probably knew who he was. Higgs says that it's not known whether Potiphar's wife liked her role as his wife or not. Maybe she was a trophy wife and liked it. Maybe she had too much time on her hands and not enough responsibilities. Higgs knows how it feels to be nameless in certain situations. She's often recognized as Matthew's mother or the driver of particular minivan.

Joseph probably knew Potiphar's wife's name. Joseph was also a handsome man and bright. He was also in a situation over his head. He was fresh from the fields and suddenly finding himself in the luxury of Egypt. Although the Bible tells readers about Joseph, Potiphar's wife remains relatively unknown. She is only present in this one scene. Potiphar's wife told Joseph to come to bed with her. She was the wife of a very powerful man and she expected to be obeyed. Joseph was just a slave and a foreigner to boot. Joseph refused because he didn't want to abuse his master's trust or God's. He saw adultery with her as a sin. Yet, Potiphar's wife continued day after day to try to seduce him.

Potiphar's wife didn't care about Joseph. One day she tried again and Joseph fled, leaving his coat behind. Potiphar's wife called to her servants and made it look like Joseph had tried to attack her. When Potiphar learned of the incident, he was angry, although the Bible doesn't say at whom. He could have killed Joseph, but he placed his servant in a prison instead.

The lessons that Christian women can learn from Potiphar's wife include staying vigilant against temptation and surrounding themselves with support. Higgs also says that women need to seek out their husbands and confess their sins when they goof up.

Chapter 3, Pillar of the Community Summary and Analysis

Lottie stands looking across Spirit Lake. The ice on the lake has hairline cracks in it and Lottie wonders where spring is. She likes the serenity of sitting out by the lake, even if her family thought she was nuts. She turns to go back to the cabin, nestled in the Cascades. She'd designed it herself and she loves it. As she starts her way back, she feels tremors under her feet. She drops to her knees at the earthquake, but when it is over, nothing seems to have changed. Above her looms Mount St. Helens.

A week later, the mountain blasts steam from its top and sulfurous gases spew out at random times. Neighbors begin saying that the government is going to make everyone evacuate from Spirit Lake. Lottie decides that they can't make her leave. She loves her house and isn't intimidated.

In May, the knock comes. Two officers come to evacuate Lottie and her family. She tries to convince them that she doesn't need to go, but they demand that she come. She tells her family to pack suitcases, and when the time comes, she again tries to stay. The officers tell her that she has to leave, so Lottie finally gets in.

Just after they get underway, Lottie remembers that she didn't take the videotape of the cabin's contents. If anything happens, she'll need that to get the insurance money. She convinces the two men to take her back, saying that she'll find the tape and follow them in her truck. The drivers finally agree and take off with Lottie's family.

Lottie has already decided that she's not going. She falls asleep on the porch, watching the mountain. In the morning, Mount St. Helens erupts and rock and ice completely overwhelm Spirit Lake. Fifty-seven people die.

Higgs writes that no one is ever prepared for disaster. Lot's wife in the Old Testament also wasn't ready. She's another of the no name Bad Girls. Although Lot and his wife look good in comparison to their neighbors in Sodom, they could have been better. Lot was selfish and he choose to bring his family to Sodom, knowing the city's bad reputation. Lot's wife probably enjoyed the trappings of their riches right along with her husband.

Abraham, Lot's uncle, pleaded with God to spare Sodom and God agreed that he would if ten righteous men could be found there. Two angels are sent to the city. Lot welcomed them into his home, but the men said they wanted to sleep in the square. Lot insisted and the angels finally agree to stay with him. That night, all the men of the city came to Lot's house and demanded the men be given to them. Lot offered his daughters instead of two visitors. The mob continued to demand the two men. The angels strike the mob blind so that they can't find the door or the men.

At this point, Lot's wife hasn't been mentioned in the Bible's account. The first mention is when the angels told Lot to take his wife and daughters and flee the city. The angels also told the family not to look back at the destruction. The Bible tells us Lot's wife's fate. She looked back and became a pillar of salt. The Bible doesn't say why Lot's wife looked back and Higgs gives several explanations. Maybe Lot's wife missed the warning or she was curious about what was happening. She may have longed for her material possessions or she may have been clinging to the past. Whatever the reason, she was killed for looking back.

Higgs argues that the lesson of this particular story is that women need to follow God's message when he tells them to go and not look back at their previous lives. The lesson teaches women that actions speak louder than words and that God's word is clear on how women should live. The escape route that women have today is through Jesus and life with him is eternal.

Chapter 4, Dying for a Drink Summary and Analysis

The men at the bar call for Crystal to bring them another drink. Her ex-husband Wayne is at the bar tonight. Crystal prefers to work during the quiet shifts when there aren't too many people or bad memories coming through the door. She is happy that tonight is pretty quiet and Wayne really isn't a problem. She wishes her ex-husband Lowell was more like Wayne or even Jimmy, who'd married again, Richard, who'd skipped town, or Bart, who'd died. She thinks that it's a good thing that Mick, her current boyfriend, isn't around to see Wayne there. Mick is jealous, although Crystal doesn't see the point of marrying him after five failed weddings.

Crystal hears the door close softly and hopes that it's not Lowell. The guy who walks in is a stranger and she figures that he's thirsty and lonely. The guy gives Crystal the creeps as he looks right at her as if he is trying to see her soul. He asks if Crystal will give him a drink and says that he'll have what she is drinking. Crystal's impatient with him, thinking that he's hitting on her. She gives him the water, charging him two dollars, the same that it would have been if he'd ordered an actual drink. He drinks it and when she asks if he liked it, he says that he's had better.

Another group of people comes in and Crystal moves to wait on them. When she turns around, the man is behind the bar, getting another glass. As a couple sits down at the bar, the stranger asks if he can give them something to drink. Crystal gives the stranger a nasty glance. Then, she notices that the stranger has given the couple water instead of the gin and tonics that they had ordered. She yells at the man, asking him what he is doing.

Crystal is surprised when the couple say the drink is the best they've ever had. The stranger pours more water for a group of fishers. She lifts the glass that the man had poured for her and is amazed at how good it tastes when she sips some. The stranger tells her that the water is life. He then tells her that he knows that she's living with a man who is not her husband and that she's had five husbands before. He asks Crystal if she'd like more to drink and she says that she would.

When Jesus was walking on earth, Jews tried to avoid Samaria. They saw the people there as less honorable. Jacob's well was in Samaria, and one day Jesus stopped there. It was probably around noon, the hottest time of the day and when people weren't likely to be there.

A Samaritan woman came to the well to get water. Jesus asked the woman for a drink, which would have been a surprise to her as Jesus was a Jew and a man. She was a social reject, yet he asked her for help. She was at the well during a time of day when others weren't likely to be about. When she questioned him, he told her that she should be asking him for living water.

The woman challenged Jesus a bit, asking him why the well water wasn't good enough for him when it had been for Jacob. He told her that drinking from the well wouldn't cure anyone from being thirsty. She asked him for his water so that she won't have to go back to the well again. Jesus told her to go get her husband and come back, which was giving her both honor and reassurance. She told him that she had no husband and Jesus said that he knows. She had had five husbands and was now with a man who wasn't her husband. In that day, many men died early from disease, warfare, and other problems, but five was still a pretty big number. However, the woman was now living with a man she wasn't married to.

The woman tried to divert attention away from her own situation, but she didn't lie or try to deny what Jesus knew. They talked a bit about religion and the woman said that she knew the Messiah was coming. Jesus told her that he was the Messiah. The woman believed. She left her water jar and ran back to the town to tell the people there. The other Samaritans from the town came with her back to Jesus. The woman's shame became a part of her past.

Higgs says that women can learn from the woman to ask questions when they don't understand. They can also recognize that not lying is not the same as telling the truth about a situation. The woman at the well also teaches women that God gives them their thirst and that when they find the water, they should share it with others.

Chapter 5, The First Cut is the Deepest Summary and Analysis

Judge Sam Nazar is sleeping in Lila's barber's chair. He came in every week for a trim and a shave. Every week while Lila did these tasks, he fell asleep. The other stylists think that it's funny that he falls asleep. Sam is a formidable man when he is awake. Lawyers and criminals fear him and there are many rumors and legends about him. One says that he killed a runaway lion at the zoo.

Sam is in love with Lila, but no one knows. Lila thinks that Sam may be her ticket to better things, although he does talk about God a lot. He doesn't buy her gifts or talk about the future either. Lila runs her fingers through Sam's hair, which he wears a little longer than any other judge. Sam always said to just take a bit off his hair and Lila now sets to work. She wishes that she'd met him years ago. As she combs his hair, she feels scar tissue underneath his hair.

When Lila touches the area, Sam jerks awake and Lila accidentally cuts him with the scissors. Although it's just a tiny wound, it bleeds. Lila apologizes and asks him about the scar. He refuses to talk about what the scar is from and finally jokes that a dog bit him.

Lila can't get the incident out of her mind. On Saturday, three men come in at closing. They say that they know Sam gets his hair trimmed every Thursday and that he sees Lila on Saturday night as well. They also know that Sam talks in his sleep and they want Lila to record him, coaxing a confession from him that he killed a man. They offer her money, enough to have the life that she wants. She decides that she has no future with Sam anyway and agrees.

Delilah was probably the last woman that a mother would choose to have her son involved with, but Samson got involved with her anyway. Samson had taken Nazirite vows and he struck fear in the hearts of his enemies. He and the Philistines had been battling for years, each trying to extract the most blood from the other.

Delilah was the woman that the Philistines would use to cut Samson down to size. The Bible says that Samson cared for her, although it doesn't say if Delilah had the same feelings. She lived in the valley between the lands of the Philistines and the Israelites and she owned her own house, which was unusual for the day. Delilah was also highly desirable. Samson must have found her very beautiful, and her name can translate to "flirt" or "coquettish woman." Although commentators often refer to her as a prostitute, there's really no evidence that she was.

Higgs argues that the best word to describe Delilah may be "pawn". She was used by the Philistines to get Samson. They told her to seduce him so they could subdue him. Their word choice indicates that they wanted to humiliate Samson before they killed him. The Philistines offered her money in exchange for Samson.

Delilah asked Samson what caused his great strength. Samson gave her several answers, but none of them proved correct when Delilah tried them. The Bible says that she nagged him for the answer. Annoyed and tired of the whining, Samson gave in and told her that if anyone cut his hair, he'd lose his strength. Delilah knew that this time he had told the truth and she sent word to the Philistines. She put him to sleep and a man shaved off his braids. Samson's strength left him.

Samson awoke to find himself tied up and unable to break free. Delilah disappears from the Bible at this point, although she remains a well-known figure from the Bible even today. The Bible does tell readers what happened to Samson though. He was led into the Philistine temple, blinded and weak. Higgs wonders if Delilah was in the audience. If she was, she would have died along with everyone else in the temple. Samson pulled down the pillars of the temple, killing everyone.

Higgs writes that the lessons women can take from Delilah are to treasure a man's love when it is given. Money doesn't make good companionship, so women need to cultivate the relationships they have. Rather than exposing the weaknesses of the people around them, women should help strengthen weaknesses and build their men up instead of cutting them down.

Chapter 6, Generous to a Fault Summary and Analysis

Sofia opens the envelop with excitement. She's been waiting years for this invitation. She calls to her husband, Aidan, and reads from the card to tell him that they've been invited to the annual awards dinner for The Three Rivers Philanthropic Society. Her mind wanders to what she'll wear and how long she should wait to accept the invitation.

Sofia and Aidan had moved to Pittsburgh twenty years ago, struggling financially. Sofia had wanted to be part of the old money scene, although they couldn't afford it then. Sofia and Aidan waited, making all the right moves in their investments and housing choices. They'd also saved over the years for the contribution of one million dollars that was expected at the awards dinner.

The next day, Aidan returns home to tell Sofia that they'd lost everything. All of their discretionary income is gone, although they still have enough to keep their home. He says that the contribution to the society will have to wait. When Sofia pushes him, saying that they'll never be asked again, Aidan concedes that they may be able to sell their West Palm Beach vacation home.

Three months later, Lila and Aidan get ready for the awards dinner. They had placed their home on the market for one million dollars, and they had actually gotten an offer for more than that. They decided that they'd give the million dollars and keep the extra, since no one would know. They arrive at the dinner and Sofia is very happy and excited. She sees Aidan go up to the second floor and she admires him as he climbs the steps. She's introduced to people from old money. She notices that all the women are dressed more plainly than she is and that they talk about charity events, but not shopping or trips.

The women hear a sound overhead and soon a man appears to get Sofia. Aidan is laying dead on the floor. Sofia notices that one of the men has the envelope that Aidan had brought and asks if that's their money. The man says that it was and that Aidan had agreed in writing to donate the entire profits from the sale of the home. He tells Sofia that he knows they got more money from the home than the money they donated. Sofia realizes that it's over and she falls to the floor beside Aidan.

Sapphira was also good with giving and lying about money. Giving was an important part of the first century church. Everyone contributed what they had to the group, almost like the communes of the 1960s. One man sold some property that he owned and gave it all to the apostles.

One couple, Sapphira and Ananias, saw the respect and praise that this act brought and decided to do the same. Higgs argues that this couple was probably well-known in the church, maybe even serving as leaders. They were followers of Christ, although that didn't stop them from lying about the donation.

Sapphira and Ananias decided to keep some of the money from the sale for themselves. Higgs says that the issue wasn't the money that they donated, but their honesty about the situation that got them in trouble. Peter knew that they were lying, although the Bible doesn't say how he knew. They were greedy and they lied. When Peter questioned him, Ananias fell down dead.

Sapphira came later to the place, not knowing what had happened earlier. Peter asked her about the money, giving her a chance to come clean. However, she continued to lie. Just as quickly, Sapphira fell down and died.

The lessons that Higgs says readers can learn from Sapphira include giving to give, not to be noticed or get praise. Greed and generosity don't mix well and Christians should be joyful givers. Women should be honest in all circumstances and examine why they want to give before they do to make sure that their motives are in the right place.

Chapter 7, Knockin' on Heaven's Door Summary and Analysis

Rae's heart beats fast as she opens the door. Four cops in plain clothes stand on her doorstep. They ask about the two men who've ducked into Rae's door. Rae tries to play innocent, but finally admits that the two men were there, leaving when they discovered her line of business. Rae tells them that the men went south and that she'd appreciate it if they left since she has someone coming. One of the cops says that women like her always are expecting someone.

The two men had knocked on her door earlier, desperate but not dangerous. They'd introduced themselves and said that they'd come from Caltech. The man are seismologists and they study earthquakes. Then the cops had arrived so she told the men to go up to the roof.

Once the cops leave, Rae comes upstairs to find the men. One of the men thanks God that she helped them. Rae asks if they know God. She tells them that a woman at the grocery store has been putting tracts in her bags. Last week, the woman had told Rae that God loved her. She tells them that she read a few verses of the Bible and found that while God hates sin, he loves people.

Rae wonders if the men know who she was and what she did. One of the men says that God sent them to San Francisco to save lives and apparently hers was first. The men tell her that they believe that an earthquake is going to hit in the next four hours. It will be a big one. They say that they prayed about what to do and God told them to tell the people. They tried to get the officials to listen, but they just sent the cops after them. Rae asks the men if they'll come back to help her before the quake hits since she doesn't have a car.

The men agree to come back for Rae and her family. They tell her to paint a big red X on her roof so that they can find her house. Rae does and several hours later the men arrive in a helicopter to save Rae. As her family starts to get on, they feel a faint tremor. One of the men looks at his watch: 5:04 p.m. on Tuesday, October 17.

Higgs says that some people are defined by the occupation that they have, and that is true for both Rae and Rahab. Rahab was a harlot, the Bible tells us. She lived by the city gates of Jericho. According to rabbinical tradition, Rahab was one of the most beautiful women.

Two Israelite spies showed up at Rahab's house one day, probably needing a place to hide while they scoped out the city. The king sent Rahab a message to bring the men out, but Rahab hid the men rather than turning them over to certain death. She told the officials that the men had come but that they'd left. Higgs argues that Rahab's actions are even more courageous because she didn't know these two men. Rahab must have sensed that they were from God. Through the men, Rahab comes to worship God, believing in him.

Rahab asked the men to spare her and her family. The men agreed to spare her if she doesn't tell anyone what's going on. She let them down by a rope through the window and told them to go hide in the hills for three days until the king's men stop looking for them. The men told her to put a scarlet cord in her window so that they'd know which house is hers.

Rahab put the cord out and gathered her family in her house. The Israelites began a siege of Jericho, which lasted seven days. The Israelites spared Rahab and her family and she went to live with them.

Higgs points out that even the New Testament writers insist on calling Rahab a prostitute, keeping her attached to the label she gave up when she turned to God. She says that stories like this, which show how God changes lives, glorify him. Some people, though, have a hard time getting beyond the labels and the past. Yet, Rahab shows that a woman's past doesn't have to determine her future. Higgs also suggests that Rahab illustrates caring for others and making a public confession. Finally, she argues that Rahab shows that faith demonstrated will be remembered by God.

Chapter 8, Friends in Low Places Summary and Analysis

Jasmine sighs when she catches her husband Abe staring at the house across the street again. Abe pines over the blue stucco building, but the owner refuses to sell it. Abe and Jasmine already own several houses on the block, so Jasmine's not sure why he thinks he needs that house.

Jasmine promises Abe that she'll get the house for him. She thinks that the land would be a nice place to greet her adoring public, who'd crowned her Queen of the Quarter. The land could be used as a new worship spot for Vodun, an ancient practice she'd adopted from her ancestors. Jasmine thinks that her religion gives her power and she wants to make her father proud as well as get Abe to quit whining about the property.

Jasmine gets on the phone and arranges for the deed to the house and a duplicate set of papers. She'd forge Abe's signature. Once the new papers were at the courthouse, she could initiate a search for the title and find Abe's name on it.

Abe smiles as he steps foot into his new home. He's not sure how Jasmine managed it, but he doesn't really care now that the house is his. He strolls through the gardens and settles on a bench. A man comes into the garden and asks what Abe did to Nate. The man says that Nate killed himself. Abe relaxes when he sees that the intruder is the street preacher in his parish. Abe thinks that the man is crazy. Abe responds that he didn't kill Nate. The preacher says that Abe has still sinned in the eyes of God and that Jasmine will be devoured by dogs. Abe calls out to God for repentance.

Years later, Jasmine has the best seat as she waits for the Mardi Gras parade to come by. Abe died long ago in an accident and now Jasmine calls the shots. Her servant brings her a drink and a few others join him. Below, Jasmine catches sight of a familiar face and leans over to show her displeasure to him. Dogs are barking below so she leans out farther to speak to the man.

Higgs writes that Jezebel is the baddest Bad Girl of the Bible. Her name has come to be a part of today's vocabulary to refer to a morally corrupt woman. She worshipped Baal and wanted to get rid of any references to God in Israel. She killed off God's prophets. The Bible doesn't refer to her as alluring or attractive and it doesn't say if her husband, King Ahab, loved her. The Bible does show that she loved money. She appears as bold, assertive, and smart. Jezebel also had strong leadership abilities. However, she used all of these things for evil. When Ahab wanted Naboth's vineyard, Jezebel set out to make it happen. She took control of the situation.

Jezebel arranged for a day of fasting where Naboth would be seated by two unscrupulous men. The men were to testify that Naboth cursed God and the king. Naboth was put to death. When Ahab went to claim his new land, he encountered Elijah, who told him that Jezebel would be devoured by dogs and dogs would lick Ahab's blood.

While Ahab repented momentarily, Jezebel did not. Even after Ahab was killed, she remained a proud Bad Girl. Two of her servants pitched Jezebel over her balcony. Horses trampled her underfoot. When they went to get her body, only the skull, hands, and feet were left.

Higgs writes that women can learn to choose their own paths in life instead of following the sinful ones of our ancestors. She also suggests that no one wants to work for a witch, as evidence by Jezebel's servants killing her. Higgs says that women should pray for a gentle, supportive spirit in their marriages.

Chapter 9, Out of Step Summary and Analysis

Michele's father yells that she can't date Dave. Michele tries to reason with him that Dave is a good worship leader in their church, but she knows that her father thinks Dave is too good and that threatens him. Rockstone Community Church had once been the biggest church in Oklahoma City, but it had been in decline until Dave came. The congregation refers to Dave as "The Music Man". Michele's father didn't like that Dave's music takes up more and more of the service. Since he believes that a service shouldn't last longer than an hour, his own sermons get shorter and shorter.

Michele continues to see Dave on the sly, until her father catches them together. After he sends Michele out to the car, her father tells Dave that she is going to marry someone else and that if Dave doesn't leave town, he'll make sure that Dave never works in ministry again. Dave agrees to leave Michele along.

After a dozen years of marriage, Michele is surprised to find that her husband Phil isn't home when she gets there. Phil doesn't give her much space. She can't believe that she'd fallen for Dave all those years ago, particularly after he father had told her that Dave was seeing her just to get brownie points with him. Dave never called again either and had left the church to begin his own music ministry. Her husband is safe and attentive. The marriage has little passion, but little pain either.

Michele turns on the television and sees Dave on the screen. Apparently, he is on tour again. Michele finally admits to herself that she still thinks about him. She thinks that he still looks good. The phone rings and she finds that it's Dave, calling to offer her a ticket to his concert in town the next night. She agrees.

Phil arrives home and Michele tells him that she's going to the concert the next night with a friend. When Phil questions her, she admits that she's never stopped thinking about Dave and how she still misses him. Phil tells her to go, but says that he doesn't know if he'll be there when she comes back.

Michele spends the next day acting like a teenager. She gets her nails done and buys a new outfit. Phil asks her not to go, but his slobbering makes it easier for Michele to walk out the door. She gets her seat at the concert and waits. Then, Dave appears on stage, but he's in a loincloth and he's dancing around. Michele feels sick. She leaves and goes home to find a note from Phil saying that he's not sure if he can forgive her.

Michal loved David. Her father was King Saul, who was jealous of David. Saul allowed Michal to marry David so that she could trap him and David could be killed. The marriage appears to have been politically motivated for David. While David loved God, Michal loved David. Saul continued to hatch plans to kill David. When Saul throws a spear at him, Michal urges David to run away and hide. She made it look like David was still in bed to give David more time to get away.

Michal suggested to Saul that David threatened her life in order to get away. After this, Michal disappears from the Bible for a bit while David marries several more women and hides from Saul. Higgs says that several chapters later Saul gives Michal to another man, maybe to punish her. Michael had no choice in the situation.

After Saul died, David became king. As David and Saul's houses continue their war, David asked for Michal to be brought to him as part of an agreement to stop the fighting. Michal is being treated like a trophy. David hasn't tried to get her in over fourteen years, but now wants her. David married more women in the years to come and Michal again drops from sight.

On the day that David brought the Ark of the Covenant to the city, David stripped off his robe and tunic and danced. Higgs writes that he probably wasn't wearing much, but that this was a way of humbling himself before God. Michal watched from a window. She despised David as he danced. She had been treated badly, but she still refused to worship God. She was jealous that other women saw what she thought they shouldn't and never gave her heart and soul to God.

Higgs suggests that Michal serves as a lesson to worship God to the fullest. Her story also shows that unconfessed sin stops worship and that angry words can hurt others and the person saying them. Finally, Michael shows women what happens when they don't rise above the circumstances.

Chapter 10, I beg Your Pardon Summary and Analysis

Anita reads the headline stating that the mayor is holding a gala at White Point Gardens. The public is invited and Anita plans to go. Half the men that will be there she's probably slept with and the rest would know her reputation. She's just been released from prison after the governor of South Carolina decided to pardon her. She puts her long hair into a French twist and puts her cologne in her purse.

Anita still can't believe that the governor pardoned her from all her crimes and all the things she'd done wrong. She wonders how she'll ever be able to thank him. She's never been good with words and she wonders how she'll dare talk to him in person.

Anita arrives at the party and scans the crowd for the governor. She moves through the crowd, trying to spot him. She wonders what she's doing there, particularly when she sees all the uniformed guards. She can't believe that she thought she'd be able to walk right up to him and shake his hand. She finally spots him, but he's with a group of people, some of whom she knows were opposed to her pardon.

Anita sees the governor's son sitting on the grass. She remembers that he has some mysterious disease that leaves him with open wounds and pain. She finds that he is looking at her. She finds herself moving toward him and she sees forgiveness in his eyes. She begins to cry and ends up with her cheek against his bare foot, with her hair falling all around.

The governor thinks to himself that Anita doesn't think he sees her. He watches as she goes to his son and begins to cry. His son had advised the governor to pardon her. The mayor asks him who is slobbering over his son and when he realizes who it is, he offers to call the police. The governor likes that she is doing this.

The sinful woman is Higgs' favorite Bad Girl in the Bible. The Bible never gives her a name or much about her other than that she had a bad reputation. She showed up at a dinner that Simon was holding and brought an alabaster jar of perfume along with her, which would have been expensive. She knew what everyone thought about her, but she wasn't going to miss seeing Jesus.

When the woman gets close to Jesus, she begins to cry on his feet. She knew that Jesus forgave her for all of her sins. She wiped his feet with her hair, which would have been almost unspeakable to those around her. A woman's hair was to be kept up. By letting it down, she was doing something that the society reserved for privacy between a man and his wife. She kissed his feet and poured the perfume on them.

The people at the dinner began talking and judging the situation. Jesus told them a parable about two men who owed money and were pardoned. The one who owed the most would be the most grateful. He then pointed out to the people that the woman had worshiped him and treated him better than any of the others there. Jesus said to her that her sins were forgiven, that her faith had saved her. He told her to go in peace.

Higgs writes that the lessons from the sinful woman include that people will always talk about others and they will often see themselves as the good guys even when they are not. She also notes that Jesus can hear pleas for forgiveness even when the person never utters a word.

Conclusion, From Bad to Verse Summary and Analysis

Higgs wonders whether the reader has found herself in any of the Bible's Bad Girls. She says that she identifies with all of them in some way or another. The common ground between the Good Girls and the Bad Girls is that they all need a savior. Their goodness won't get them into heaven and their badness won't keep them out. Christ can save both.

Higgs reminds the reader that God loves her. She also says that she appreciates the reader herself. Higgs and her readers, along with other Christian women, can use the wisdom from the Bad Girls to become better Christians. She includes a short poem that lists all of the Bad Girls in the book and says that God has the power to change their lives if they ask.

Important People

Eve

Eve is the first woman that God created. When God saw that Adam needed a companion, he took a rib from Adam and created a woman. Adam and Eve lived in the Garden of Eden, peacefully with the animals and being able to talk to God. Higgs suggests that Eve had to be beautiful since she wouldn't have had blemishes or scars. She was also sinless when she was created, so her personality would have been the best possible.

A serpent came to Eve and talked with her about the trees in the garden. Eve told him that they were not to eat from the fruit that came from the tree at the center of the garden. The serpent tells Eve that she will have greater knowledge if she eats the fruit. Although the serpent had planted the seed, Eve could have resisted the temptation at several points. Instead, she took her focus off God and put it on the tree. She ate the fruit and offered it to Adam as well. Their eyes were open to the reality of sin as soon as they did.

Potiphar's Wife

Potiphar is the king's head of security in Egypt. However, Potiphar is more concerned with eating than he is with his wife. The Bible doesn't give much information about Potiphar's wife beyond the one scene that she appears in. The reader isn't told how she feels about Potiphar or what she looks like.

Potiphar's wife decides that she wants to sleep with Joseph, one of her husband's slaves. Joseph believes that this would be a sin and would break the trust that his master and God have in him. He turns Potiphar's wife down. She continues to ask him to sleep with her and he continues to refuse. One day, she sends everyone out and tries again. When Joseph runs out, she grabs his coat and tells everyone that Joseph tried to attack her. Joseph is sent to prison because of her actions.

Lot's Wife

The Bible gives little information about Lot's wife, not even her name. The story tells the reader that Lot choose to live near Sodom, a city that he knew was full of sin. When God decides to wipe out Sodom and its sinful citizens, Lot's uncle pleads to spare the city if ten righteous men can be found there. The angels sent do not find that number and they tell Lot and his family to escape before it's too late. The family is commanded not to look back at Sodom. Yet, as they escape, Lot's wife looks back and is turned into a pillar of salt.

Higgs discusses the fact that the Bible doesn't say why Lot's wife looked back. She offers several suggestions including that Lot's wife didn't hear the warning, dropped something, or heard a cry for help. Lot's wife may have been mourning the loss of her possessions or longing for the things that she had to leave behind. Higgs suggests that God tried to lead Lot and his family to safety, away from their destructive lifestyle, but Lot's wife didn't trust him. She was disobedient, foolish, and stubborn. Higgs states that Lot's wife should be a reminder to all women to take God's hand and walk with him instantly when asked.

The Woman at the Well

The woman at the well lived in Samaria. She came to the well in the heat of the day, which Higgs argues she did to escape the wagging tongues of the other women of the town. The woman had been married five times and was currently living with a man who was not her husband. The women meets Jesus at the well. He knows her background without her having to tell him. When he tells her that he is the Messiah, she believes him instantly. She runs off to the town to tell everyone. Her neighbors believe her account, coming to meet Jesus for themselves.

Higgs suggests that the woman at the well is an example of a woman who has been bad for a season. She is living with a man who is not her husband and she tries to conceal the truth from Jesus when he asks her about it. However, the woman chooses to accept Jesus when she realizes that he is the Messiah. She turns from her Bad Girl ways and focuses her attention on God. Higgs also argues that she serves as an example of how ministry should be. The woman hears the good news and instantly goes to share it with others.

Delilah

Delilah is a woman who lives between the Philistines and the Israelites. She becomes involved with Samson. The Philistines offer her money in exchange for finding out how to subdue Samson's strength so that they can humiliate and kill him. Delilah agrees and sets out to learn Samson's secret. She is angry when he lies to her several times about how to subdue him and begins to nag him until he finally breaks down and tells her. She arranges it so the Philistines can shave his hair, rendering Samson weak. She collects her money.

Higgs suggests that Delilah must have been a very beautiful woman who knew how to manipulate men. Although the Bible says that Samson loved her, it gives no indication about how she felt about him. In the end, she chooses money over Samson. Higgs also wonders if Delilah went to the Philistine temple the day that the men dragged Samson in. If so, she would have died along with everyone else there. Higgs argues that Delilah offers an example of how not to relate to the men in one's life.

Sapphira

Sapphira is an example of how a woman can go bad for a moment with devastating effects. She is a part of the first century church and Higgs suggests that she may be a leader in the church. When she and her husband see the praise and respect given to someone who donates the money from a land sale, they decide to do the same. However, they only give a portion of the sale, telling everyone that it is the full amount. Peter confronts the couple one at a time and each one continues to lie. Both Sapphira and her husband die suddenly after lying to Peter.

Higgs argues that Sapphira took her eyes off God, focusing instead on her own greed and selfishness. In many other ways, Sapphira is a Good Girl. She's a part of the early church and is following Jesus. However, she tries to give for the wrong reasons. Instead of giving to God, she gives to get recognition and praise. Although the Bible doesn't say what Sapphira dies of, the circumstances suggest that both Sapphira and her husband die because of their lies.

Rahab

Rahab is a prostitute who lived in Jericho. Two Israelite spies show up on her doorstep one day and she hides them from the king's men, who want to kill the spies. Rahab recognizes God through the men and believes. She helps them get out of the city and to safety. The men tell Rahab to put a scarlet cord in her window so that the Israelites will recognize where she lives and save her when they overtake the city.

Rae is another reformed Bad Girl in the Bible. She comes to believe in God and turns away from her sinful ways. After the Israelites overtake the city and kill the other inhabitants, Rahab goes to live with the Israelites.

Jezebel

Jezebel is the Bible's ultimate Bad Girl. She is married to King Ahab and worships Baal. Throughout her life, Jezebel continues to choose evil and sin over God. She has God's prophets killed and promotes the worship of Baal. When Ahab covets a vineyard but the owner won't sell it to him, Jezebel takes matters into her own hands. She arranges it so that the owner of the vineyard will be implicated for cursing both God and the king in front of witnesses. The owner is killed because of the accusations and Ahab gets his vineyard. The Bible says that even when confronted with her sin, she remains proud and unrepentant.

The prophet Elijah tells Ahab that Jezebel will be devoured by dogs for her wickedness. Several years later, Jezebel is thrown to her death by several of her servants. She is trampled by horses and dogs eat her body. Only her skull, hands, and feet are left.

Michal

Michal is King Saul's daughter and she loves David. David wants to marry Michal, although it seems like more of a political union than one of feeling. Saul tries to use the relationship to kill David at several different points, although his attempts are unsuccessful. When Saul becomes more explicit in his threat, Michal urges David to hide. She covers up David's absence to give him more time to get away. In the next few years, David marries several other women and Saul gives Michal in marriage to another man, even though she is already married to David.

Years later, David asks for Michal as part of an agreement with Saul's family. She comes back to him, but is disgusted with him when he dances practically naked in front of his people while worshiping God. Higgs writes that Michal loves David more than she loved God, which causes her to oppose his worship of God.

The Sinful Woman

The sinful woman is another of the Bible's Bad Girls who is not named. She shows up at Simon's dinner party with an alabaster jar of perfume. The perfume is expensive, but she wants to honor Jesus with it. She washes his feet with her tears and dries them with her hair. The other people there are scandalized by her behavior, but Jesus forgives her sins.

Ruthie

Ruthie is the fictional character who represents Higgs' own past. In the introduction, Ruthie has started dating a man who begins to abuse her. Although she tries to get away, the man manages to get inside her apartment. Higgs would eventually leave the situation and find God.

Evelyn

Evelyn is the fictional character for the story of Eve. The story finds her on the night of her debutante ball, where she will later become engaged. The ball is being held at the home she shares with her father. Her father has asked Evelyn to stay away from the gazebo at the center of the garden. Evelyn allows a man named Devin to take her to the gazebo where he kisses her. She later kisses her fiance, with both of them losing their innocence and purity with the kiss.

Mitzi

Mitzi is the fictional character for Potiphar's wife. Mitzi's husband ignores her, so she hatches a plan to seduce a young man from her husband's office. She calls the man and gets him to come over to get something, but when he gets there, she tries to put the moves on him. When he resists and leaves, she decides to cover her tracks by making it look like the man tried to take advantage of her.

Lottie

Lottie lives by Spirit Lake in the shadow of Mount St. Helen. When the mountain threatens to erupt, Lottie doesn't want to leave her beloved home. She engineers a way to remain behind when the evacuation orders come, thinking that the worst won't happen. In the end, Lottie is killed because she wouldn't leave her possessions. Lottie represents a modern interpretation of Lot's wife.

Crystal

Crystal works in a bar and people gossip about her, as she's been married five times and is now living with another man. One night, a man comes into the bar and offers Crystal the water of life. Although she resists at first, she ultimately drinks the water and asks for more. She is the fictional equivalent to the woman at the well.

Lila

Lila is the fictional account of Delilah. Lila works in a barber shop and she cuts Judge Sam Nazar's hair each week and gives him a shave. Lila is also having a secret relationship with Sam, yet he doesn't talk about the future and wants to keep everything quiet. Several men offer Lila money if she'll record the things Sam says in his sleep. They believe that he killed someone and want to get a confession on tape. Lila agrees to help them in exchange for money.

Sofia

Sofia is the fictional representation of Sapphira. Sofia wants to be a part of the old money society. She convinces her husband to donate one million dollars so that she can join an exclusive awards dinner and gain recognition. After they receive their invitation, they lose a great deal of money and have to sell their vacation home in order to still attend the dinner. They agree to give the full purchase price of the home to the charity, but when they receive more than one million, they decide to keep the difference. However, someone at the charity knows that they received more and confronts them.

Rae

Rae is a prostitute in San Francisco and she is the fictional representation for Rahab. She gives refuge to two men who are trying to warn the city about a coming earthquake. She hides them from the police. She asks them about God and comes to believe in God. The men agree to come back to save Rae and her family. She paints a red X on her roof and the men come in a helicopter to get Rae and the family that has gathered.

Jasmine

Jasmine is the fictional account for Jezebel. Her husband wants a neighboring home, but the owner won't sell it to him. Jasmine forges the deed and papers for the house to make it look like her husband owns the house. Even after the owner commits suicide, Jasmine doesn't repent. She dies years later when she falls out of a balcony.

Michele

Michele is the fictional character for Michal. Michele secretly dated a man named David, although her father didn't want her to. Her father eventually finds out and tells lies to both Michele and David about each other so that they stop seeing each other. David leaves town and Michele marries Phil, who her father approves of. Years later, David calls to invite Michele to see him in concert. She agrees and tells her husband that she still misses David. However, when she goes to the concert, she's embarrassed by David's actions and leaves, only to find that Phil has left her.

Anita

Anita is the fictional account for the sinful woman. Anita has just been pardoned by the governor for her crimes. She hears about a reception for the governor and decides to attend to show him her gratitude. She takes some expensive perfume with her. When she gets there, she begins to approach the governor, but sees his son. The governor's son has a mysterious illness that often scares people away. Anita goes to him and sees that he forgives her. She cries over his feet and wipes them with her long hair.

Objects/Places

The Gazebo

Evelyn is told by her father to avoid the gazebo. She allows Devin to take her there, knowing that she is disobeying her father.

The Garden of Eden

Adam and Eve lived here after God created them. They eat the fruit from the tree that God commanded them not to in the garden.

The Tree of the Knowledge of Good and Evil

God told Adam and Even not to eat of the fruit from this tree. They disobey God and eat the fruit anyway.

Egypt

Joseph encounters Potiphar's wife when he was living in Egypt.

Spirit Lake

Lottie lives by Spirit Lake. She refuses to leave when Mount St. Helens threatens to erupt and is killed when it does.

Sodom

Lot and his wife live in this town, which is full of evil people. As they flee from the city, Lot's wife looks back and is turned into a pillar of salt.

Sychar, Samaria

Jesus meets the woman at the well at this town. Many in the town come to believe in Jesus through the woman.

The Valley of Sorek

Delilah lives in this place, which is between the Israelite and Philistine lands.

Philistine Temple

After Samson's hair is cut and he loses his strength, the Philistines take him to their temple to "perform". Samson pulls down the pillars of the temple, killing everyone inside.

Jericho

Rahab lived in Jericho. She put out a scarlet cord in her window so that the Israelites will save her and her family.

Nate's House

Abe Kingsbury wants Nate's house for his own. Jasmine forges the papers so that she can give Nate's house to him.

Naboth's Vineyard

King Ahab covets Naboth's vineyard, but can't get Naboth to give it to him. Jezebel arranges it so Naboth is killed. She and King Ahab take over the property.

White Point Gardens

Anita visits a party at White Point Gardens to show her gratitude to the governor for pardoning her. She ends up washing the feet of the governor's son.

Simon's Dinner

The sinful woman attends Simon's dinner. She washes Jesus's feet with perfume and dries his feet with her hair.

Themes

Choice

One of the themes throughout Bad Girls of the Bible is choice. Higgs argues that each person has the choice to be a Bad Girl or a Good Girl in their life. The free will that God gave people allows women to choose to act in ways that are Christlike or to act in ways that are not. The choices that a woman makes in her life help determine whether a woman is bad for her lifetime, a season, or just for a moment.

An aspect that comes out of the discussion of choice is that every woman is susceptible to bad moments. Even women who follow Christ and believe in God are tempted. Higgs shows how those moments of temptation can lead women into actions that forever change their lives. Eve gives in to the temptation of eating the forbidden fruit, bringing sin into the world. Lot's wife gives in to the temptation of looking back, turning her into a pile of salt. Sapphira, a believer in the early church, gives in to the temptation of greed and lying, which kills her. These women may have lived exemplary lives up until that point, but they each look away from God and onto something sinful.

The discussion of choice that Higgs has brings out the idea that women need to be constantly on guard for the temptations in their lives. Women have the choice to resist temptation and follow God or to give in and look away from God. Although some of the women in the chapters choose temptation repeatedly, others either did not or they turned away from their sins and toward God. As Higgs points out, a number of the Bad Girls of the Bible are women who choose Christ in the end over their previous sinful lives. In those situations, God transformed their lives into something better.

Bad Girls

As the title indicates, Bad Girls of the Bible is about Bad Girls, those women who choose sin, looked away from God, and messed up in their lives. Higgs argues that these women have much to teach today's women. Although the Bible has Good Girls (Mary and Esther, for example), the Bad Girls offer a different perspective on finding God and how to remain faithful. As Higgs states, all women have been Bad Girls at some point or another because women are human and they sin.

From the very start of the book, Higgs identifies herself as a reformed Bad Girl. She clearly states that she has things in her own past that she's not proud of, but that God saved her from her Bad Girl past and put her on the road to salvation. Higgs argues that because all women are Bad Girls at some point in time, they may find it easier to identify with the Bad Girls than the Good Girls of the Bible. It can be hard to measure oneself to someone who is always good and faithful when one has sins, mistakes, and doubts. The Bad Girls illustrate that God loves everyone, regardless of what they have done, and that he offers salvation to Bad Girls as well as the Good Girls.

Higgs breaks down the Bad Girls of her book into several different categories. First, she identifies the women who are bad to the bone. Jezebel is one example of this type of Bad Girl. Her heart is hardened against God and she constantly chooses sin over him. Second, Higgs says that there are women who are bad for a season. These are the women who have a past, but who choose God and change their ways. The woman at the well, Rahab, and the sinful woman are all examples of women who have been bad for a season, but have opened their hearts to God and become reformed Bad Girls. The final category that Higgs discusses are the women who are bad for a moment. These are the women who follow God, but who give in to a moment of temptation. Lot's wife is one example of a woman who is bad for a moment. She choose to look away from God and toward her former home, when she's been commanded not to, just for a moment. Yet, that moment is enough to seal her fate.

God's Love

Throughout the book, Higgs argues that the Bad Girls of the Bible have much to teach women about God's love. Even though each of the women Higgs discusses is bad, at least for a time, God always offers them the chance to change and follow him. He is always present in their lives and puts people in their path who could help them change. Even Jezebel, one of the ultimate Bad Girls, has the prophet Elijah to show her the way, if she only wanted to follow God.

Higgs includes several examples of women who turned from their sinful ways to live with God. These include Rahab, the woman at the well, and the sinful woman. Each of these women is identified in the Bible as being sinful, often through their sexuality. Yet, even though their society labeled them as sinful and outcasts because of their actions, God still choose to redeem them. These three women instantly realize who God is when they encounter him and decide to follow him, giving up their former sins.

Higgs includes these women as well as her own story to illustrate God's love and concern for all women. God accepts even the outcasts when they come to him for salvation. While a woman may be bad for a moment or a season, she doesn't have to be bad to the bone. Higgs argues that God can soften even the hardest heart when a woman looks to him and away from her sin.

Style

Perspective

Liz Curtis Higgs is a nationally known writer and speaker. She has written several fiction and non-fiction books. She states at several points that she has a past that was sinful until she met Christ. Although she doesn't give specifics about her past, she says that it included drugs, sex, and other earthly temptations. She is now married and has several children.

Bad Girls of the Bible began as Higgs was researching women of the Bible for a talk she was giving at a national conference. She found that she identified with and related to the Bad Girls of the Bible more than the Good Girls of the Bible. She says in the introduction that she wants women to know that they are not alone. She writes for several different types of women: former Bad Girls who are trying to fit in with God's family, temporary Bad Girls who have put aside their devotion, veteran Good Girls who want to understand other women, and aspiring Good Girls who think that there's more to life and want to find it.

Higgs aims the book for both personal devotion and group study. She believes that many women have encountered sin in their lives and can find comfort and lessons in the stories of the Bad Girls. She weaves together her own thoughts on the women with Biblical commentaries to help find lessons in each of the women's lives.

Tone

The tone of Bad Girls of the Bible is very accessible. Higgs wants women from various backgrounds and places in life to receive the lessons that the women's stories have to offer. She uses both fictional and non-fictional accounts of the stories to further that, drawing in women who prefer one or the other.

Although knowledgeable about the topic, Higgs doesn't present herself as the ultimate authority. She draws from other scholars and religious leaders to construct a picture of the women she discusses. She also often gives differing points of view or speculates about the context of the story when it's not present. For example, when she discusses Lot's wife, she offers a number of suggestions for why she may have looked back. At the same time, Higgs is writing from a religious viewpoint, so she does assume that certain behaviors are bad when others may not have the same opinion.

The overall tone of the book works for the type of book that Higgs is writing. The sometimes humorous commentary and Higgs' accessible writing style makes the book a good choice for religious study groups and for women reading on their own. The tone is aimed for an adult female audience for the most part.

Structure

Higgs separates Bad Girls of the Bible into ten chapters, with each chapter focusing on a different Bad Girl. Higgs also includes an introduction, conclusion, study guide, and notes. In the study guide, Higgs includes additional verses that her readers can go to for more teaching on the themes from the chapters.

In each chapter, Higgs opens with a fictional, modern account that resembles the Biblical story. After that, she discusses the Biblical story of the particular Bad Girl. Higgs weaves together the verses from the Bible with her own thoughts and the commentary of other scholars. She often speculates about parts of the story that the Bible doesn't include. At the end of each chapter, Higgs includes four lessons that can be learned from the story and discussion questions that can be used by book discussion groups or individuals for themselves.

The structure of the book works well for the aims that Higgs has for the book. The inclusion of the discussion questions makes the book easier for groups to use in discussion groups or Bible studies. The focus on one woman per chapter also allows Higgs to pull out some of the details and context for the reader, giving more perspective on what was happening.

Quotes

"It all boils down to a heart that's hardened against God--however temporary the condition, however isolated the tough spot.

"To that extent, we've all been Bad Girls." Introduction, p. 4

"I have trouble learning, though, from women who get it all right. I spend my energy comparing, falling short, and asking myself, How do they do that? It's discouraging, even maddening. It also doesn't get me one step closer to God." Introduction, p. 4

"Funny: The older scholars blamed the women for everything and painted the men as heroes. The newer writers blamed the men for everything and described the women as victims and the men as jerks. The truth lies somewhere in the middle, so that's what I aimed for: balance. And truth." Introduction, p. 6

"The tree that had been in the middle of everything yet obediently avoided-- for how long we don't know--suddenly, that tree was it. The all-consuming, gotta-have-it thing. Like a child of Christmas past who put only one item on her wish list--cabbage Patch Doll, Tickle-Me Elmo, Beanie Baby--Eve had a fixation about that tree." Chap. 1, p. 29

"The entire axis of human history rotated on six words: 'She took some and ate it.'" Chap. 1, p. 32

"The Lord used Mrs. Lot's story to make a point. When he returns, we are to be ready to follow without hesitation, forsaking everything. Salvation is offered freely but at a price: our old lives in exchange for new lives in Christ." Chap. 3, p. 81

"Oh, it gives me shivers just to think of it! The Lord reaching out to someone who was in all ways a social reject. Notice he didn't command her; he asked her. His words were polite and forthright, the start of a lengthy conversation--the longest found in Scripture between Jesus and anyone, let alone a Samaritan." Chap. 4, p. 92

"Maybe it was the fear of not having enough--enough money, enough recognition, or enough of what she might have hoped those things would buy her: love. We hoard when we fear loss. We can all live without stuff. None of us can live without love. When we see someone demanding attention, as Sapphira did, it's a sure bet that what's needed isn't wealth, fame, or applause. It's love." Chap. 6, p. 141

"Rahab's sins were as scarlet as the thread that draped from her window, and every bit as obvious. Oh, can I identify with that! That's why God's grace is so amazing. When we confess our sins--literally let them all hang out like Rahab's red thread--and repent, leaving the old life behind as Rahab did, we are forgiven and washed clean, without a spot or blemish left." Chap. 7, p. 161

"With God, it isn't who you were that matters; it's who you are becoming." Chap. 7, p. 165

"Potiphar's wife loved men. Delilah loved money. Jezebel loved power."
Chap. 8, p. 178

"Jezebel stands out because she was a gifted woman who had every opportunity for greatness. Instead, she threw her chances out the window to embrace a foreign god who--when push came to shove--couldn't save one of his most devoted followers from a terrible end." Chap. 8, p. 185

"Since Jesus knew everything about this quiet worshiper, perhaps she had already given up her life of sin. After all, the evidence of a changed heart was kneeling at his feet. Without a word, she expressed repentance. Without a sound, she cried out for forgiveness. Without a syllable, she spelled out the desire of her heart: to love him. Her actions said it all." Chap. 10, p. 231

"Worship is about rekindling an ashen heart into a blazing fire." Chap. 10, p. 232

"And did you discover the common denominator, other than our womanly roles as daughters, wives, mothers, and friends? It's simply this: Good Girls and Bad Girls both need a Savior. The goodness of your present life can't open the doors of heaven for you. The badness of your past life can't keep you out either. Not if you truly desire the forgiveness and freedom Christ offers." Conclusion, p. 237

Topics for Discussion

Which of the Bad Girls do you relate to the most? Why?

What is the most important lesson that you learned from the Bad Girls of the Bible? How can you apply this lesson to your own life?

Why do you think God spared Lot and his family? Do you think they deserved to be saved? Why do you think Lot's wife looked back when she was being saved from the destruction?

Why do you think the nameless women aren't named in the Bible? Do you think that this makes their stories more or less powerful?

Several of the chapters discuss women who are judged by those around them. Why are they judged? Have you ever been judged by others? How did you feel and how did you handle the situation? What can you learn from the women in the Bible who were judged?

Why is Jezebel the ultimate Bad Girl? What does she do to earn this title? Does she have any good qualities?

In the stories about Potiphar's wife and Michal, the women's husbands are focused elsewhere. Do you think the men loved their wives? How did the men's actions affect the women? Do the men's actions (or lack of them) absolve the women of responsibility for their actions? Who is to blame in these situations?

Higgs categorizes the women as being bad to the bone, bad for a season, or bad for a moment. What does she mean by these labels? Give an example of a woman in each category? How do the categories differ in their approaches to God?

Made in the USA
Coppell, TX
28 August 2023

20890687R00042